Extreme Downhill BMX Moves

By Mary Firestone

Consultant:
Keith Mulligan
Editor / Photographer
Transworld BMX Magazine

CAPSTONE
HIGH-INTEREST
BOOKS

an imprint of Capstone Press
Mankato, Minnesota

Capstone High-Interest Books are published by Capstone Press
151 Good Counsel Drive, P.O. Box 669, Mankato, Minnesota 56002
http://www.capstone-press.com

Library of Congress Cataloging-in-Publication Data
Firestone, Mary.
    Extreme downhill BMX moves / by Mary Firestone.
    p. cm.—(Behind the moves)
Summary: Discusses the sport of extreme downhill bicycle motocross
racing, describing some of the jumping and passing techniques as well
as safety concerns.
    Includes bibliographical references and index.
    ISBN 0-7368-2152-X (hardcover)
    1. Bicycle motocross—Juvenile literature. 2. Extreme
sports—Juvenile literature. [1. Bicycle motocross. 2. Extreme sports.]
I. Title. II. Series.
GV1049.3 .F57 2004
796.6'2—dc21   2002155467

Editorial Credits

James Anderson, editor; Jason Knudson, book designer; Jo Miller, photo
    researcher; Karen Risch, product planning editor

Photo Credits

AP/Wide World Photos, 4
Digital Vision Ltd., 10(inset)
Keith Mulligan/Transworld BMX, cover, 7, 8, 10, 13, 14, 16, 18, 20, 21, 22, 23,
    25, 26, 29
PhotoDisc, Inc., 4(inset), 18(inset), 26(inset)

Table of Contents

Learn about:

X Games

Bike frames

Obstacles

Chapter One

Downhill BMX

On August 12, 2001, BMX riders Robbie Miranda and Brandon Meadows sped down a hill at Woodward Camp. Miranda and Meadows were racing in the downhill BMX main event at the 2001 Summer X Games. Miranda was ahead of Meadows as they rounded the last berm.

As Miranda jumped a huge double at the end of the race, his back tire caught the dirt. He spun out. He bounced on the ground and crashed. He was just a few feet from the finish line. Brandon Meadows won the race and the gold medal.

Robbie Miranda did not give up. He kept training and went on to win the gold medal at the 2002 Summer X Games.

History

Bicycle Motocross (BMX) racing started in the 1970s. The first BMX riders built dirt tracks in their backyards. They were copying motocross. This motorcycle racing sport takes place on a dirt track.

Today, BMX racing is organized. BMX riders compete at local, national, and international events.

The first downhill BMX event was at the 2000 Vans Triple Crown. Since then, the TV network ESPN has hosted downhill BMX races at the Summer X Games.

Equipment

Any 20-inch (51-centimeter) bike can be used in a BMX race if it has padding on the handlebars, stem, and frame. Most downhill BMX riders prefer bikes made for BMX racing.

Downhill BMX racing bikes are made of chromoly steel. Chromoly is a steel alloy. It is made of two metals called chromium and molybdenum.

Chromoly frames are strong and heavy. During a downhill BMX race, riders land hard from 40-foot (12-meter) jumps. Even sturdy chromoly bikes can get destroyed in a tough race.

BMX racers use tires called knobbies. These wide tires have a thick tread that gets traction in the dirt. The tires grip the dirt surface well. Good traction is important for turning and pedaling faster. Traction also reduces slips and spinouts.

Even knobbie tires can go flat.

Downhill tracks have many steep obstacles.

Downhill BMX bikes have a single hand brake that riders use for stopping or slowing down. The brake helps control the momentum of a bike. Momentum is the force or speed that a bike has when it is moving.

The Downhill BMX Track

Most downhill BMX tracks are about 1,500 feet (460 meters) long. Downhill BMX tracks have obstacles and straightaways.

BMX tracks have four kinds of obstacles. They are doubles, step-ups, step-downs and tabletops. Doubles are two same-size jumps in a row. A step-up is one jump over two hills. The first hill is lower than the second. A step-down is also a jump over two hills. The first hill in a step-down is higher than the second. A tabletop is a jump with a flat top.

Straightaways are clear areas of a track. There are no obstacles or turns on straightaways.

A race begins when the gate falls.

Learn about:

Balancing on the gate

Berm lines

Passing

Chapter Two

Downhill BMX Moves

Downhill BMX races are quick. They last only about 40 seconds. Riders race in groups of eight or less. Each race is called a moto. Racers usually take practice runs through the track before the race.

Starting

At race time, riders line up at the starting gate. A race official calls out, "Racers ready!" This is a sign that the race is about to start.

The riders stand up on their pedals and balance while they wait for the gate to fall. This move is called "balancing on the gate." Starting on the pedals helps riders take off to a fast start.

When the gate drops, riders pedal fast. Riders try to take the lead from the start. They find it much harder to take the lead later by passing other riders. Collisions and crashes are common as riders try to pass.

Berms

In downhill BMX racing, almost all turns have berms. A berm is the banked curve on a track. In order to pass other riders and win races, BMX racers must become skilled at riding berms.

Each berm has three imaginary turn lines. They are called the outside, middle, and inside lines. Racers who take a turn wide are riding the top edge of the berm. The top of the berm is the outside line. The middle line runs through the center of the berm. If a rider takes the inside line, they are on the bottom of the berm.

Most riders prefer to take the inside line. This means they enter at the bottom and quickly swoop up to the top of the turn.

Riders can enter any line on the berm, or exit on any line. Riders rarely follow the same line through the turn.

Riders swoop to the top as they enter a berm.

Passing is dangerous at 40 miles (64 kilometers) per hour.

Passing

Downhill BMX racers are aggressive about passing. Racers can use their elbows and knees to nudge their way through other riders, or to keep other riders from passing. Downhill BMX riders also can move directly in front of racers. They try to force the other rider to slow down, or they may collide.

Riders who pass on a straightaway must pedal fast. Riders must have strong leg muscles to overtake other riders on straightaways.

Passing in downhill BMX racing is dangerous. Riders are moving at up to 40 miles (64 kilometers) per hour. A failed pass can knock down other racers. If riders collide high in the air over a jump, they can be seriously injured.

Extreme Downhill BMX Slang

backside—the downhill side of a jump that a rider lands on

bail—to jump off a bike to avoid a crash

case—not getting both wheels to the backside of a jump when landing

catching air—a high leap off or over a jump

endo—falling over the handlebars of a bike

rad— something cool, crazy, or awesome

sucking-up the lip—staying low and pushing down off the lip of a jump

swoop—to take an inside line and quickly move to the outside line on a berm

Gravity provides momentum in downhill races.

Learn about:

■ Momentum

■ Casing a jump

■ Staying low

18

Chapter Three

Extreme Downhill BMX Moves

Gravity provides riders with momentum in a downhill BMX race. Riders pedal very little, except at the beginning, and on straightaways.

Momentum

If riders pedal too fast, they could go over a jump with too much momentum. Too much momentum can cause riders to lose speed or crash when they land.

Downhill BMX riders also are careful about going too slow. Racers need to pedal to create enough momentum to get over a jump.

Riders stay low during jumps.

Jumps

Downhill BMX racers do not do any tricks during the race. They do not try to get high in the air during a jump. Racers try to stay low during jumps. This helps them remain balanced for the hard landings.

If riders jump high in the air, they try not to "case" the jump. Casing is when a wheel does not make it over a jump. Casing a jump can slow riders down or cause them to fall. Riders who fall or lose momentum in downhill races usually will not win the race.

Riders are careful not to case a jump.

Sucking-up the lip

When riders jump off an obstacle, they "suck-up the lip." Sucking-up the lip is remaining low and pushing the bike down off the lip of the jump. Sucking-up the lip helps riders keep from going too high in the air.

Riders push down off the lip of a jump.

Getting Backside

Downhill riders try to "get backside" on doubles. They land high on the backside of the jump. Racers who land higher on the backside of a jump build more momentum for the next jump. When riders get more backside it also means less pedaling for the next obstacle.

Some downhill jumps are called blind jumps. Riders cannot see the landing until they are in the air. Riders get a chance to take these jumps during practice runs. During the race, they remember where to find the landing.

Riders have to remember landings on blind jumps.

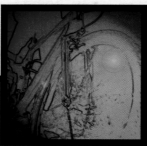 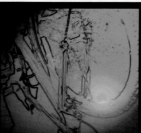 

Learn about:

Pads

Full-face helmets

Falling

Safety

Downhill BMX racing is a dangerous sport. Riders race closely in groups and crashes are common. Riders get hurt often, but they can do several things to protect themselves during a race.

Padding, Clothing, and Helmets
BMX bike frames are padded on the handlebars, stem, and top tube. The padding keeps the rider from landing on hard bike metal during a fall.

All downhill BMX racers must wear long sleeves, long pants, and a full-face helmet. Gloves are also a good idea. Pro riders also wear jerseys with elbow pads and padded racing pants to protect themselves.

Safe Riding

Downhill BMX racers practice how to fall safely. If they fall during a race, they try to fall away from their bikes. They roll with the fall instead of landing hard in one place.

Riders keep their arms and legs in a bent position at all times during the race. Bent arms and legs act as shock absorbers for bumpy rides. This position also allows a rider to quickly jump from the bike during a fall.

Practicing is important for a beginning downhill BMX racer. Practice will improve the rider's skills and prevent falls. Practice is the only way to perfect the extreme moves in downhill BMX racing.

All downhill riders wear full-face helmets.

Words to Know

berm (BURM)—a banked turn or corner on a BMX track

chromoly (KROH-mol-ee)—a mixture of two metals called chromium and molybdenum; this material also is called "chromo."

double (DUH-buhl)—two same-size jumps in a row

obstacle (OB-stuh-kuhl)—an object that stands in a rider's way; jumps are obstacles.

step-down (STEP-doun)—a jump made of two hills, the first one higher than the second

step-up (STEP-uhp)—a jump made of two hills, the first one lower than the second

tabletop (TAY-buhl-top)—a jump with a flat top

To Learn More

Blomquist, Christopher. *BMX in the X Games.* A Kid's Guide to the X Games. New York: PowerKids Press, 2003.

Tomlinson, Joe. *Extreme Sports: The Illustrated Guide to Maximum Adrenaline Thrills.* New York: Carlton Books, 2002.

Young, Ian. *X Games: Action Sports Grab the Spotlight.* High Five Reading. Mankato, Minn.: Capstone Press, 2002.

Useful Addresses

American Bicycle Association
P.O. Box 718
Chandler, AZ 85244

Canadian BMX Association
P.O. Box 2080
Grand Forks, BC V0H 1H0
Canada

National Bicycle League
3958 Brown Park Drive
Suite D
Hilliard, OH 43026

Internet Sites

Do you want to find out more about downhill BMX?
Let FactHound, our fact-finding hound dog, do the research
for you.

Here's how:

1) Visit *http://www.facthound.com*
2) Type in the **Book ID** number: **073682152X**
3) Click on **FETCH IT**.

**FactHound will fetch Internet sites picked by our editors
just for you!**

Index